NFL TEAM STORIES

The Story of the
DETROIT LIONS

By Craig Ellenport

Kaleidoscope
Minneapolis, MN

The Quest for Discovery Never Ends

....

This edition first published in 2021 by Kaleidoscope Publishing, Inc.

No part of this publication may be reproduced in whole or in part without written permission of the publisher.

For information regarding permission, write to
Kaleidoscope Publishing, Inc.
6012 Blue Circle Drive
Minnetonka, MN 55343

Library of Congress Control Number
2020933887

ISBN
978-1-64519-228-2 (library bound)
978-1-64519-296-1 (ebook)

Text copyright © 2021 by Kaleidoscope Publishing, Inc. All-Star Sports, Bigfoot Books, and associated logos are trademarks and/or registered trademarks of Kaleidoscope Publishing, Inc.

Printed in the United States of America.

Bigfoot lurks within one of the images in this book. It's up to you to find him!

TABLE OF CONTENTS

Kickoff! 4

Chapter 1: Lions History 6

Chapter 2: Lions All-Time Greats 16

Chapter 3: Lions Superstars 22

Beyond the Book 28
Research Ninja 29
Further Resources 30
Glossary 31
Index 32
Photo Credits 32
About the Author 32

KICKOFF!

Detroit companies make a lot of cars. They have built trucks, sports cars, and station wagons. The cars put Detroit on the map as the "Motor City." The city's football team is the Detroit Lions. Just like the car companies, the Lions make the city proud. The Lions have not been champs for a while. Still, they have thrilled fans with exciting players. Let's find out more about this great NFL team.

Chapter 1
Lions History

Football has a long history in Detroit. In the 1920s, the Motor City had four NFL teams. The first was the Detroit Heralds in 1920. They were later called the Tigers. The Detroit Panthers played in 1925 and 1926. The Wolverines were a 1928 team. None of those teams stuck around.

In 1930, the NFL's Spartans began play in Portsmouth, Ohio. In 1934, they moved to Detroit. The Spartans became the Lions!

In 1935, the Lions won their first NFL championship! They defeated the New York Giants to win the title. Detroit's leader was Hall of Fame quarterback Earl "Dutch" Clark.

Lions players in white leather helmets battled the Chicago Bears in 1935.

In the 1950s, Detroit was one of the NFL's best teams. The Lions won the NFL title three times. They were the champs in 1952, 1953, and 1957. They beat the Cleveland Browns each time! In 1954, the Lions made the NFL Championship Game, but the Browns beat them.

LIONS AND TURKEYS

The Lions play every year on Thanksgiving. The tradition began in 1934. G.A. Richards owned the Lions. He wanted something special for his new city. He got the Chicago Bears to come to town. The Bears spoiled the party! Chicago won 19-16. Richards liked the idea, though. Since 1945, the Lions have hosted a game on Thanksgiving Day every year.

A Lions fan shows off his turkey hat at a Thanksgiving Day game.

The Browns (in white) tried to stop the Lions from winning the 1953 title.

The Detroit stars were QB Bobby Layne and running back Doak Walker. Layne and Walker were good friends. Long before playing for the Lions, they were teammates in high school. Layne was one of the NFL's best passers. Walker was a powerful runner. Together, they made the Lions' engine go!

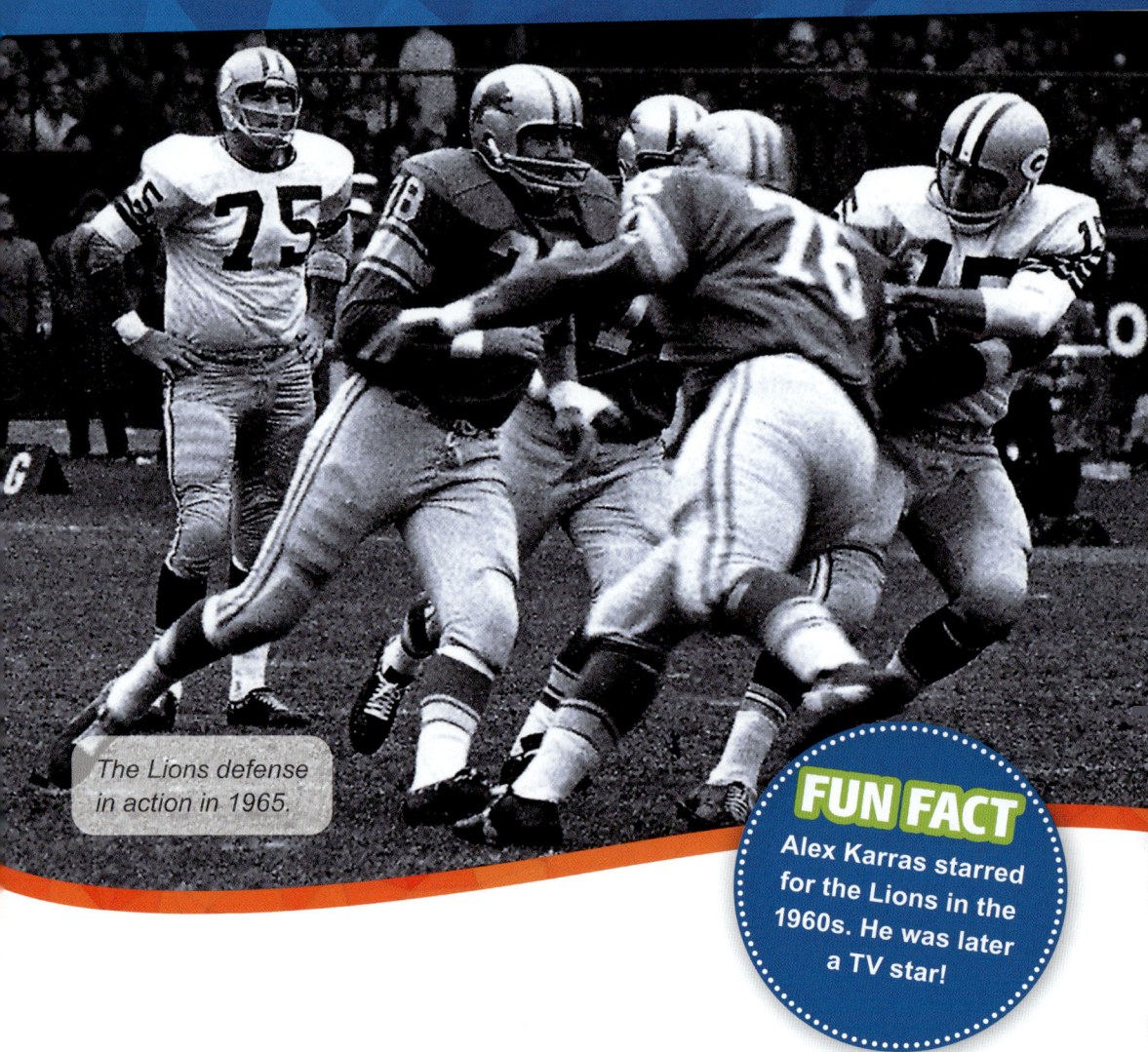

The Lions defense in action in 1965.

FUN FACT
Alex Karras starred for the Lions in the 1960s. He was later a TV star!

The Lions had a **winning record** five times in the 1960s. They never made the playoffs, but they were tough to beat. Detroit had one of the best defenses in the NFL. It was in the top 10 every year. The leader was middle linebacker Joe Schmidt. Schmidt's position was pretty new in football. His talent made the idea permanent. Schmidt was smart and fierce.

Joe Schmidt

In 1970, the Lions made the playoffs, but lost in the first round to the Dallas Cowboys. Detroit went to the playoffs twice in the 1980s.

In 1989, the Lions **drafted** running back Barry Sanders. Sanders was one of the greatest running backs in NFL history. Thanks mostly to Sanders, Detroit went to the playoffs six times in the 1990s.

In 1991, the Lions won 12 games. That was a team record. In 1995, their offense was ranked number one in the league. They made the playoffs for the third year in a row.

Barry Sanders

TIMELINE OF THE DETROIT LIONS

1935

1935: The Lions beat the New York Giants, 26-7, to win their first NFL title.

1953

1953: Detroit wins the NFL Championship for the second year in a row. Both wins were against the Cleveland Browns.

1957

1957: The Lions win their fourth NFL Championship. They beat the Cleveland Browns, 59-14.

1970

1970: Detroit reaches the playoffs for the first time since 1957. They lose a close game to the Dallas Cowboys, 5-0.

1991

1991: The Lions win a team-record 12 games. They lose to the Redskins in the NFC Championship Game.

2014

2014: In Jim Caldwell's first season as head coach, Detroit finishes 11-5 and makes the playoffs.

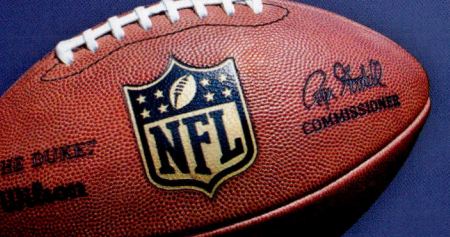

CHAMPIONS!

The Lions' last championship was a surprise. It was 1957. Late in the season, Bobby Layne broke his ankle. Detroit's star was out! Tobin Rote took his place. Could the backup win the big games?

Detroit finished tied for first place in its division. The Lions had to break the tie. They played the San Francisco 49ers. The 49ers led by 20 points in the second half. The Lions were not done. They roared back! Tom Tracy dove in for a 1-yard touchdown. Then Tracy ran 58 yards for another score. In the fourth quarter, Gene Gedman ran for a TD. The Lions were ahead! They added a field goal and won 31–27.

In the NFL Championship Game, they played the Browns. Rote took control. He threw four touchdown passes. He also ran for a score. The Lions won 59-14!

The Lions' 1950s plastic helmets were much thinner than today's high-tech models. The face masks were smaller, too!

Hall of Fame running back John Henry Johnson scores for Detroit.

Chapter 2
Lions All-Time Greats

Fifteen Lions players have made it to the Pro Football Hall of Fame. Dutch Clark was the first. In the 1930s, Clark was listed as a quarterback. His talent was not passing, it was running. He led the NFL in rushing touchdowns three times.

FUN FACT
Clark was also a Lions kicker! He made 15 field goals and 72 extra points.

Bobby Layne

In the 1940s, Detroit's best players were Alex Wojciechowicz and Bill Dudley. Wojciechowicz played center on offense. Then he played linebacker on defense. In those days, many players played "both ways."

In the 1950s, QB Bobby Layne led the way. He set many NFL passing records. He was also a great leader. Running back Doak Walker made the **Pro Bowl** five times.

Detroit's Barry Sanders was one of the greatest backs in NFL history. Sanders was super quick and hard to tackle. A tackler would line him up. Then Sanders would spin past. Another tackler approached. Sanders stopped! The tackler flew past and Sanders kept running. He was amazing!

Sanders played for 10 seasons. He gained at least 1,000 yards in all of them.

Barry Sanders

FUN FACT: Sanders is fourth all-time on the NFL's rushing list.

Wide receiver Herman Moore starred with Sanders. Moore was taller than most receivers. That helped him catch balls other players couldn't. In 1995, Moore set an NFL record with 123 catches.

Receiver Calvin Johnson broke many of Moore's team records. Johnson was big, strong, and fast. His nickname was "Megatron." In 2012, Johnson set an NFL season record for most receiving yards.

Herman Moore

LIONS
RECORDS

These players piled up the best stats in Lions history. The numbers are career records through the 2019 season.

Total TDs: Barry Sanders, 109

TD Passes: Matthew Stafford, 256

Passing Yards: Matthew Stafford, 41,025

Rushing Yards: Barry Sanders, 15,269

Receptions: Calvin Johnson, 731

Points: Jason Hanson, 2,150

Sacks: Robert Porcher, 95.5

Chapter 3
Lions Superstars

Today's Lions are led by QB Matthew Stafford. Stafford passes for a lot of yards and touchdowns. He is also a great leader. He makes sure his teammates are working together. Detroit is never out of a game with Stafford on the field. Stafford holds team records for passing yards and touchdowns.

Stafford is tough and **reliable**. He started every game for the Lions from 2011 through 2018. In each of those seasons, he topped 4,200 passing yards. His career best came in 2011. He threw for an incredible 5,038 yards! At the time, it was the third most for a season in NFL history.

Matthew Stafford

Kenny Golladay

Stafford has good targets for his passes. Marvin Jones Jr. has been a reliable receiver. In 2017, he gained about 18 yards per catch. That was best in the NFL.

Kenny Golladay joined Detroit in 2017. He has become one of the NFL's top receivers. In 2019, he led the NFL with 11 touchdown catches.

TIE IT UP!

During the regular season, NFL games can end in ties. Tied teams play one overtime period. If the score stays the same after that, the game goes as a tie! Detroit tied Arizona 27–27 to start the 2019 season!

Marvin Jones Jr.

Detroit's running game is powered by Kerryon Johnson. He has topped the Lions in rushing yards in both of his first two NFL seasons. Johnson is young, but very quick. He gives Stafford a target out of the backfield, too.

Kerryon Johnson

Detroit's defense is led by Mike Daniels and Trey Flowers. They play on the defensive line. Daniels has the speed to chase down quarterbacks. His best skill is stopping running backs up the middle. Flowers plays defensive end. He uses his speed and power to sack the quarterback. Flowers had 7 sacks for the Lions in 2019.

Detroit has a long history of great players. Today's fans are watching some of them. Will those stars "drive" another title to the Motor City?

Trey Flowers makes a big tackle.

BEYOND THE BOOK

After reading the book, it's time to think about what you learned. Try the following exercises to jumpstart your ideas.

RESEARCH

FIND OUT MORE. Where would you go to find out more about your favorite NFL teams and players? Check out NFL.com, of course. Each team also has its own website. What other sports information sites can you find? See if you can find other cool facts about your favorite team.

CREATE

GET ARTISTIC. Each NFL team has a logo. The Lions logo shows a lion, of course! Get some art materials and try designing your own Lions logo. Or create a new team and make a logo for it. What colors would you choose? How would you draw the mascot?

DISCOVER

GO DEEP! This book writes about the Lions toughest seasons. There have been a lot lately. Read more about the team and its fans. How do they stay excited after all the losses? How would you feel if your team lost year after year? What can the Lions do to improve?

GROW

GET OUT AND PLAY! You don't need to be in the NFL to enjoy football. You just need a football and some friends. Play touch or tag football. Or you can hang cloth flags from your belt; grab the belt and make the "tackle." See who has the best arm to be quarterback. Who is the best receiver? Who can run the fastest? Time to play football!

RESEARCH NINJA

Visit *www.ninjaresearcher.com/2282* to learn how to take your research skills and book report writing to the next level!

RESEARCH

DIGITAL LITERACY TOOLS

SEARCH LIKE A PRO
Learn about how to use search engines to find useful websites.

FACT OR FAKE?
Discover how you can tell a trusted website from an untrustworthy resource.

TEXT DETECTIVE
Explore how to zero in on the information you need most.

SHOW YOUR WORK
Research responsibly—learn how to cite sources.

WRITE

GET TO THE POINT
Learn how to express your main ideas.

PLAN OF ATTACK
Learn prewriting exercises and create an outline.

DOWNLOADABLE REPORT FORMS

Further Resources

BOOKS

Levit, Joe. *Football's G.O.A.T. (Greatest of All Time)*. Minneapolis: Lerner Publications, 2019.

Meier, William. *Detroit Lions (Inside the NFL)*. Minneapolis: Abdo, 2019.

Payment, Simone. *Calvin "Megatron" Johnson: Superstar Wide Receiver*. New York: Rosen Education, 2019.

WEBSITES

FACTSURFER

Factsurfer.com gives you a safe, fun way to find more information.

1. Go to www.factsurfer.com.
2. Enter "Detroit Lions" into the search box and click 🔍
3. Select your book cover to see a list of related websites.

Glossary

backup: a player who replaces a starting player. Jeff Driskel is the backup to starting QB Matthew Stafford.

drafted: chosen in the NFL's annual selection of college players. Detroit drafted cornberback Jeff Okudah with the third overall pick in 2020.

Pro Bowl: the NFL's annual all-star game. Kenny Golladay's great 2019 season earned him a spot in his first Pro Bowl.

reliable: consistently excellent and trustworthy. Matthew Stafford's great arm makes him a reliable passer.

winning record: when a team wins more games than it loses. The Lions' last winning record came in 2017 when they were 9–7.

Index

Clark, Earl "Dutch," 6, 16
Cleveland Browns, 8, 14
Dallas Cowboys, 12
Daniels, Mike, 27
Detroit Heralds, 6
Detroit Panthers, 6
Detroit Wolverines, 6
Dudley, Bill, 17
Flowers, Trey, 27
Gedman, Gene, 14
Golladay, Keny, 25
Johnson, Calvin "Megatron," 20
Johnson, Kerryon, 26
Jones, Marvin Jr., 25
Layne, Bobby, 9, 14, 17
Moore, Herman, 20
"Motor City," 4, 6, 27
New York Giants, 6
Portsmouth Spartans, 6
Richards, G.A., 8
Rote, Tobin, 14
San Francisco 49ers, 14
Sanders, Barry, 12, 18, 20
Schmidt, Joe, 10
Stafford, Matthew, 22, 25, 26
Tracy, Tom, 14
Walker, Doak, 9, 17
Wojciechowicz, Alex, 17

PHOTO CREDITS

The images in this book are reproduced through the courtesy of: AP Images: Tony Tomsic 6; 14, 18. Focus on Football: 8, 9, 12, 16, 17, 19, 20, 22, 25, 26. Newscom: Terry Gilliam/MCT 10; Zach Bollinger/Icon SW 11, 24, 27. Shutterstock: Dedan Photography 4.
Cover: Focus on Football

About the Author

Craig Ellenport, a freelance writer who resides in Massapequa, New York, has written several kids books about the National Football League.